I0056822

Time-Tested Investment Sales Principles

That Will Turn You Into a World-Class Fundraiser

THE DAKOTA WAY

GUI COSTIN

WITH

MORGAN HOLYCROSS

LIONCREST
PUBLISHING

THE DAKOTA WAY
*Time-Tested Principles That Will Turn You
Into a World-Class Fundraiser*

FIRST EDITION

ISBN   978-1-5445-4710-7   *Hardcover*
          978-1-5445-4709-1   *Paperback*
          978-1-5445-4711-4   *Ebook*

Fundraising is a very difficult job. It requires a fundraiser to commit to a lifetime of "setting up meetings" during which they take a complex story and simplify it so it can be understood and retold.

Which isn't exactly what anyone went to college for.

So this book is dedicated to my industry colleagues, those hardworking women and men who are grinding away, sending emails, getting rejected, setting up meetings, doing the meetings, and eventually raising capital for their funds.

Here's to you all! Keep grinding!

CONTENTS

INTRODUCTION

When my business partner and I started Dakota in 2006, we only had the two of us as salespeople. We continued with that model for the next five years, and then in 2011, we hired our first salesperson, Tim Dolan.

Like many organizations, however, we lacked a sales training program with clearly spelled-out processes, procedures, and expectations. Instead, I trained our first employee with the Read My Mind method—I expected Tim to follow my example and achieve the same results, without any formal guidance from me or anyone else.

Unsurprisingly, my method failed miserably. Tim and the people we hired after him didn't know what they should be doing. They had no structure or guidelines. The Read My Mind training program resulted in a lot of frustration and a lot of employee turnover.

After burning through numerous salespeople over the next year, I realized I needed to do something. I needed a system of processes and procedures that I could use to train salespeople and they could all follow on their own.

So I did some research and came across a book called *Work the System* by Sam Carpenter. Sam was running a call center in Portland, Oregon, and was burned out from working too many hours. In response, he decided to document everything he did and then set the company up, through processes and procedures, so it functioned without him having to go into the office.

I decided to follow Sam's plan. I documented every single thing I did as a salesperson, from the initial outreach, to winning the mandate, and everything in between. I then started teaching that approach to each new hire.

What I learned from Sam Carpenter completely transformed our business. This method has now been codified as The Dakota Way.

THE DAKOTA WAY

In investment sales, we have what I call the Problem of Eighteen Months: as fundraisers we have eighteen months to prove ourselves or we'll be looking for another job. However, without formal sales training, new fundraising hires usually spend the first six months simply figuring out the job, who they should call on, how they should pitch the product, how to follow-up, and so on. By the time they get settled, they only have a year to make something happen—that is, to raise money—and with six- to thirty-six-month sales cycles, that strategy is problematic, to say the least. (Ideally, they need to be building pipelines in the first month, not in month nine or beyond, but I don't want to get ahead of myself.)

During those first six months spent learning the ropes, they've usually produced no sales, and they have an anemic pipeline. In response, senior leadership becomes frustrated and people get fired.

This might be a slight generalization, but it's not far off and way too sad.

I've been there. I've faced the challenges of connecting with prospects, of standing out in a ridiculously competitive market, of striving to meet and exceed unrealistic quotas, of living under the threat of changing jobs every eighteen months. During the first seventeen years of my career, I worked for eight different companies. Every eighteen months, I came home and told my wife I was leaving one job and starting another. Thankfully, she was super supportive, but changing so often had a negative impact on my early career. I never stayed in a job long enough to build a commission stream.

My first goal in writing this book is to help you overcome the Problem of Eighteen Months. I want to give you a time-tested, proven framework for effectively raising money as an investment salesperson from your first day on the job. Through this framework, The Dakota Way, you will understand what truly works in this industry: the art of setting expectations, the science of creating a Total Addressable Market (TAM), the fun of becoming a master messenger, and the leverage of a killer follow-up system (a.k.a. using a Customer Relationship Management system [CRM]).

These are the elements that, when combined, lead to

better outcomes not just in terms of raising capital, but also in maximizing your efficiency and effectiveness as a sales professional. We're talking about 10X-ing your time, achieving more with less, and reaching heights you previously thought unattainable.

My second goal is to end the massive amount of turnover that results from the Problem of Eighteen Months. That kind of churn isn't good for the individual, and it's not good for the company. It takes a while to build momentum in investment sales, and if you switch jobs every eighteen months, your forward progress keeps getting cut off. You never get the pipeline built or gain the experience, the knowledge of your product isn't developed to where it should be, and reward in the form of healthy commissions is not received. It's like pumping water in a well up to 60 or 80 percent, quitting, moving to another well, and starting all over again at zero. A lot of work with nothing to show for it.

I want to help salespeople like you stay long enough to pump water all the way out of the ground and reap the rewards of your labor. If you have the tools from day one, you will more likely pump 100 percent on your first try, stay with the company for the long haul, and enjoy a very lucrative career.

This book lays out a time-tested system for succeeding in investment sales. The Dakota Way is far more than a sales technique; it's a philosophy and a process, as well as a mindset that has been meticulously codified into four core principles:

1. Set Expectations
2. Know Who to Call On
3. Become a Master Messenger
4. Have a Killer Follow-Up System

These four principles all fall under one umbrella concept: Focus on What Matters Most. This core value is the north star of our firm and underlies everything we do. When confused or uncertain about something, we simply ask, "What truly matters here more than anything else?" Then we act on that.

These principles aren't just abstract concepts; they're the bedrock of our sales course uniquely tailored for investment sales professionals. It's the only course of its kind, designed by fundraisers, for fundraisers, who aim not just to meet their fundraising goals but to exceed them in ways they never thought possible.

As you turn these pages, you'll find detailed explanations of each of the four core principles, examples of how they can be applied, and practical exercises to help you integrate them into your own sales business. You'll learn how to prioritize your actions, focus on what truly matters most, and build a sales process that is not only efficient but also sustainable and scalable. The four core principles form a circle that when applied just keeps repeating itself.

No matter what investment firm you work for, no matter what kind of sales training is (or is not) in place, no matter how many years you've been in this industry, following this framework can and will help. Don't think of this process as a straightjacket meant to replace your individuality with a rigid one-size-fits-all solution. Think of these four foundational principles as rocks and pebbles in a jar, around which you pour the sand of your personal touch and experiences that make the methodology uniquely yours. Rather than limiting you, implementing The Dakota Way into your daily routines will leverage your natural strengths with proven strategies.

I would not use these principles at Dakota or put them here in print if I didn't truly believe they helped my team play at the highest professional level, achieve results, and stay in their careers for a long period of time.

Altogether, this handbook can guide every step of your career in investment sales, from new fundraising hire to the CEO.

LESSONS FROM THE COURSE

Between 2011 and 2018, around the same time I was formulating and first implementing The Dakota Way, I had the privilege of coaching the Haverford School golf team in Haverford, Pennsylvania. Our achievements include six league titles and two undefeated seasons, which speaks volumes to the power of teamwork and leadership. My tenure as a coach was marked by incredible victories, heartfelt connections with the team and their families, and invaluable lessons in leadership and guidance.

Reflecting on my coaching days, I realize that my role was less about teaching and directing, as a football or lacrosse coach would do. It was more about offering unwavering support and guidance. Since golf is an individual sport, everyone has their own style. I felt my job was to create a culture where each person could play unencumbered by a coach in their head.

From ensuring the team had top-notch gear to organizing memorable events for the team and families, my aim was to create an atmosphere where each player felt supported and understood. I created a structured environment where athletes could thrive by focusing on consistency, goal setting, and continuous improvement—an environment that fostered a mutual respect, allowing me to step back and let the players' talents shine.

At Haverford, I was tasked with creating a program, not just a team, and that meant encouraging focus and discipline in my athletes, crafting a process for both them and myself that was designed to lay the groundwork for this season and the ones to come.

This experience, I've come to realize, shares profound parallels with the principles of The Dakota Way. Much like the coaching philosophy I employed at Haverford, The Dakota Way establishes a program—a process that sales professionals can rely on, one that is about more than just the end results. Fundraising is a consultative sale, an educational process—not a closing style of sales like ABC (Always Be Closing). Like coaching, it's about building a culture where continuous learning, resilience, and a commitment to excellence are valued above all else. It involves creating a supportive environment where sales professionals are encouraged to focus on the things that matter most, for example, booking meetings with the appropriate end buyers, practicing their pitches for the real meeting, and ingraining the use of a CRM into their practices.

Balancing support with clear expectations was the cornerstone of my role as a coach at Haverford and continues to be my leadership approach at Dakota. It underscores the belief that when individuals feel supported and valued, they are more likely to excel and contribute positively to the organization's overall success and, of course, their own.

Yelling, demeaning, teasing, throwing people into the deep end with no help, failing to set proper expectations—these may have been common leadership tactics in the past, but they don't work. They have no place in coaching, leading, or the way we treat our teammates, fellow salespeople, or ourselves. The Dakota Way represents a departure from those old ways of treating people and brings a more humane and vulnerable approach to helping individuals get what they want out of their job and profession.

It was not always this way with my leadership style, as many of the early employees can attest. Through a process of self reflection, my own style has evolved and I've shifted my focus to helping others get what they want out of life. I'm still learning and growing.

As a nod to the lessons I learned on the course and at Dakota, I will end each chapter with a leadership note—a way to apply The Dakota Way as a leader. If you're not currently in a leadership role, that's okay. These tips will be there when you need them.

TRANSFORMATION STARTS NOW

In the dynamic world of investment sales, success is not just about what you sell but how you sell it. The Dakota

Way capitalizes on this truth and outlines a processes-driven approach to fundraising that has worked for Dakota since our founding in 2006 and has made many salespeople highly productive. It has been the cornerstone of our company's strategy, enabling us to raise over $35 billion in our partnerships with over eight investment firms—a testament to a system that's not just theory but practice, not just ideas but results.

The Dakota Way is not a quick fix or a shortcut, nor is it limited to one skill level. It's a comprehensive, long-term strategy that requires commitment, discipline, and a willingness to learn and adapt. Any investment sales professional at any point in their career can benefit from applying its principles. Whether you're a seasoned professional looking to refine your approach or a newcomer eager to make your mark in the world of investment sales, this book is the ultimate resource for you to take your career to the next level and master the art of investment sales.

Sales is not merely a goal but the culmination of numerous right actions, from the initial targeting of a prospect to getting the call that you have won the mandate. It's a long series of small things that when all stitched together create the results—the magic. The heart of The Dakota Way transcends the conventional wisdom of investment sales in order to create a structure that achieves this magic day in and day out.

We invite you to join us on this journey. Delve into strategies and insights that promise not only to enhance your sales career now but to transform your approach to leadership in the years to come. Embrace the principles, practice the techniques, and start achieving the kind of results you've always dreamed of.

Welcome to a journey of discovery, growth, and unparalleled achievement, where the ultimate goal is to elevate the standard of excellence in the fundraising business.

Welcome to The Dakota Way.

1

THE UMBRELLA—FOCUS ON WHAT MATTERS MOST

In investment sales, the landscape is perpetually shifting, presenting a myriad of challenges and opportunities at every turn. Many variables are subject to external forces far beyond our control as salespeople—market conditions, the performance of specific strategies, lack of return of private equity capital, dominating performance of just seven stocks, and the timing of investment searches are all subject to external forces, to name just a few. We have to figure out how to ignore all this noise.

In The Dakota Way, we rely on one umbrella concept to do this: Focus on What Matters Most.

This overarching idea serves as the bedrock upon which all other strategies and tactics are built, guiding sales professionals through the complexities of their roles with clarity and purpose. It emphasizes the power of focusing on factors that are within our grasp: outreach efforts, the number of meetings secured, the messages conveyed in those meetings, and the manner in which follow-up happens. Each of these elements is a lever that can be pulled to drive progress and achieve results. By focusing on controllable factors, you can ignore the uncertainties and background noise of the market, knowing that you are doing everything within your power to do the things that matter most.

In investment sales, what matters most can be distilled into the four core principles of The Dakota Way:

- Set Expectations
- Know Who to Call On
- Become a Master Messenger
- Have a Killer Follow-Up System

We will devote one chapter to each of these principles, but for now, we set the foundation: effectively using your time so that you are focusing on these areas that matter most.

TIME: THE INVALUABLE ASSET

Time, often referred to as the only asset we truly possess, is an invaluable and irreplaceable resource that dictates the pace and direction of our personal and professional lives. Time's finite nature underscores the critical importance of managing it with the utmost care and precision, especially in the fast-paced, results-oriented world of sales. Because time flies, we must Focus on What Matters Most, day in and day out.

To make the best use of our time, we must discern the

relative value of our daily activities, recognizing that not all tasks are created equal. This discernment allows us to prioritize activities that offer the highest potential return on investment, thereby propelling us forward in our goals, while avoiding those that detract from our progress.

However, the challenge lies in the ability to accurately identify which activities are truly high-impact and which are not. This requires a combination of self-awareness, goal clarity, and the ability to objectively assess your actions: Are they really bringing you closer to your sales goals? Is there a more efficient way to achieve the same outcome?

This is where The Dakota Way can help. It lays out exactly what you should be doing—as frustrating as that might be—and helps you focus on working smarter by leveraging tools and technologies that can automate routine tasks like sending invitations to schedule meetings or using Slack to get the meetings you have scheduled into your CRM. Using CRMs like this frees up more time for activities that require a personal touch—tasks that benefit from your unique skills and expertise like cold emailing or doing face-to-face meetings.

At the end of the day, the ultimate goal for a sales professional is to continuously set up meetings with qualified buyers. Thus, high-impact activities include those that directly contribute to that end, such as identifying your TAM, practicing your pitch, and city scheduling—all of which will be discussed in coming chapters. Any time spent on other activities, like redesigning the pitch deck, redesigning the website, or sending long, multiparagraph emails that no one reads, is time wasted and money lost.

By focusing on these high-value activities, you can ensure that you and your team are using their time where it matters most. Adopting this mindset permits sales professionals to ensure that they are not just busy but productive, making the most of the only true asset at their disposal: time.

NO EASY BUTTON

About thirteen years ago, one of the partners of a firm we work with announced, "We really need to redo our presentation deck."

"I'm good with that," the CEO said. "But let's be clear about one thing. We manage money, and with that presentation deck, we've raised $10 billion. I don't think it's the presentation deck that raised us the money; it's our performance. That's what matters most."

It's so natural to want to focus on things like the presentation deck, isn't it? Or rearranging your desk. Or redoing the website. Those things are so much easier to deal with than the constant rejection that comes with sales. I'm sure you get tired of unanswered emails and hearing the word *no*.

Let me say this in the nicest way possible: there is no easy button in investment sales.

There is no way around cold calling and cold emailing, and the rejection that comes with it. You have to do the hard work. Focusing on things that don't matter may be a welcome distraction, but it will not make you a successful salesperson.

In any endeavor, there are only a few things that really matter. If you focus on those key principles, everything else will fall into place. If you focus on tasks outside of these principles—like redoing the website or updating the presentation deck—you set yourself up for challenges.

As we delve deeper into the principles of The Dakota Way, you will see that this approach is not merely about selling more effectively; it's about working smarter, not harder. It's about recognizing that our time and energy are finite resources that must be wielded with precision and intent.

By focusing on what matters most through setting expectations, knowing who to call on, being a master messenger, and having a killer follow-up system, we set the stage for unparalleled success.

This chapter has laid the foundation for the transformative journey that lies ahead. Let this concept guide your actions, inform your decisions, and inspire your aspirations as you navigate the challenging yet rewarding path of investment sales.

As we explore the four core principles of The Dakota Way, remember that the journey to mastery begins with a single step: the decision to focus on what truly matters.

Now that the foundation has been laid, let's get into the first principle: Set Expectations.

2

PRINCIPLE 1—SET EXPECTATIONS

Back in 2013, Dakota was hired by one of the best invest-ment firms in the world to market a new mutual fund they had recently launched. We were late to interview for the opportunity, so when we got hired, we didn't know much about the product inside the mutual fund or any historical fundraising data about this asset class.

About a quarter into the engagement, our contact at the investment firm called. "How is the fundraising going?" he asked me. "And why don't you have more opportunities in the pipeline?"

I started to explain where we were, but realized I needed data to back up my assertions.

First, I asked for a meeting with the big boss, and then I went to work researching this particular asset class. In short, this is one of the oldest asset classes in the mutual fund industry with mutual funds dating back forty years.

With mutual funds, all the data is public, so doing an

analysis was very easy. My goal was to figure out where the majority of the assets were located and the length of their track record—meaning how long each of the largest funds had been in the market. I learned that 98.5 percent of all assets were in mutual funds that had a ten-plus-year track record, which translates to "It will take a very long time to grow this mutual fund, far beyond your patience level or projections."

When I presented this conclusion to the big boss, she looked at me and asked, "Then why did we launch this fund?"

Since we were here late to the game, I said, "I have no idea. I don't think anyone researched the asset class. This will be a very long haul with little chance of success."

Unfortunately, this is a common scenario. Many investment strategies are launched without any research on similar past funds, and no conversation takes place between the sales team and the executive team to determine What Success Looks Like. The meeting starts, and the boss says something like, "We have to raise a billion dollars!" when that's never been done for a firm of their size and based upon their investment strategy. Maybe $200 million would be a home run.

The truth is, there will always be a gulf between what the boss believes is a realistic fundraising goal and what is reality. If a sales plan is not created and agreed upon, there will always be a difference between what the boss (portfolio manager, CIO, CEO) believes is success and what the salesperson delivers.

That's why you, the salesperson, need to embrace this first principle and Set Expectations.

Sitting down to set expectations with your boss transcends the simple act of sharing information; it is fundamentally about crafting a unified sales plan to create transparency. This ultimately leads to an agreement on What Success Looks Like.

The larger the investment firm, the more likely you'll have structure around performance expectations and mandated sales plans. As you move toward the boutiques or the one-person sales teams, not so much. At these smaller companies, salespeople such as yourself often need to take initiative to give yourself structure and achievement metrics. Without structure—that is, without agreement or alignment on What Success Looks Like—the Problem of Eighteen Months rears its ugly head. If you're winging it or following the Read My Mind method, you're probably not going to be around too long.

Don't underestimate the importance of this principle. It's easy to overlook the simplicity of setting expectations and agreeing on what "good" looks like, but it needs to be the starting place. How do you know how to succeed at your job if you don't know what your boss expects of you? You have nothing to compare your actions to.

Even if you are a one-person sales team, you can put processes in place to protect you from yourself—processes that force you to create a plan and report against it. In this chapter, we'll discuss how.

WHAT SUCCESS LOOKS LIKE

There are certain things in the investment business that will never change. One of them is the fact that there's a big difference between the expectations of a PM/CEO/CIO regarding fundraising possibilities and what is actually realistic for a salesperson.

So how do you solve this difference? It requires a harmonized approach to agreeing on What Success Looks Like.

When I began documenting The Dakota Way, I had a conversation with Andrew O'Shea, a long-time partner and investment sales professional at Dakota. I mentioned the three ideas I had come up with, and he said, "Gui, don't forget the most important pillar."

I asked him, "Am I missing something?"

He said, "We have been doing this a long time, raising capital for multiple firms, and setting expectations on What Success Looks Like is the key factor in a successful relationship."

He was absolutely right. Setting proper expectations around things like the number of daily/weekly calls, number of sent emails, number of meetings set up, and how activity against accounts will be tracked is the key to a successful relationship with your boss, or in our case, our fundraising partners. This not only creates alignment and clarifies a forward path, but it also transforms your sales plan from a mere aggregation of to-dos into a uniformed transparent plan of action. Everyone is on the same page regarding what needs to be done, how to do it, and by when, which makes it much easier to track on-target performance or underperformance.

At Dakota, we say that setting expectations means you're the dog, not the tail—you're taking charge and controlling the relationship instead of following along. If you find yourself as the tail, you will likely find yourself no longer with this company.

Here's another way to look at it: if you don't set proper expectations, you are like a rudderless ship. You may end up where you need to be, but you don't have the control you need to get there as quickly and efficiently as possible.

So how do you set clear expectations upfront? By creating a simple one-page sales plan.

CRAFTING THE SALES PLAN: A BLUEPRINT FOR SUCCESS

In short, a sales plan is a narrative backed up by facts that explain exactly what you plan to do. For example, if you plan to reach out to all registered investment advisors (RIAs) and family offices, you would create a narrative that explains exactly how you'll engage with these interested channels on a daily and weekly basis. The sales plan should have as much detail as possible in terms of daily outreach, profiling these channels, and managing your pipeline. Based upon your asset class, it is also helpful to include the amount that other firms and funds like yours have recently raised, giving some reality to the plan.

The final piece to the puzzle is to include the day and time each week or every other week that you will report against the plan. This is key: if you come to an agreement on What Success Looks Like and are reporting your progress regularly against the plan, you keep yourself honest and keep your boss completely in the loop the entire way. No surprises. The worst situation you can put yourself in is having your higher ups or partners thinking you aren't doing anything.

At Dakota we have a daily check-in at 8:00 a.m. for our sales team to report on their plan and exactly what they are doing. Some may think this is a little crazy, but we have found that this daily accountability generates such a strong foundation that you cannot physically deviate from the plan even if you tried. This intense structure forces each salesperson to state how they performed yesterday against their plan and their plan for the day ahead. Ultimately, it leads to transparency between them and their boss.

Ready to create your own plan? First, think about the following questions:

- What are the primary and secondary target channels that will be interested in my product structure?
- How will I take action daily to penetrate these targeted accounts?
- How will I track my activity against these accounts to provide updates to my boss and portfolio manager?
- How often will I review my progress against the sales plan with my boss and portfolio manager?
- What is a realistic timeline to raise money for this product?

Next, think about the metrics you'll include, for example:

- Activity metrics: number of daily/weekly calls, emails, and meetings set up

- Pipeline metrics: number of accounts in each stage of the sales cycle
- Market penetration: percentage of your TAM (RIAs, broker-dealers, etc.)
- Sales cycle metrics: average time to move an account from initial contract to closing (make sure to compare this to industry benchmarks, which you'll find through asset class studies)
- Performance tracking: weekly performance against your sales plan
- Scorecard metrics: track status of key accounts and next steps

Then bring it all together into a one-page document with clearly defined sections. Here's how a sales plan for the ABC Large-Cap Growth Fund might look:

1. **Strategy Name and Product Structure:**
   - Strategy Name: ABC Large-Cap Growth Fund
   - Product Structure: Open-end mutual fund focused on large-cap growth equities.
2. **Target Channels:** The focus will be on RIAs as the primary channel, with secondary channels including broker dealers, wirehouses, and institutional consultants.
   - Primary Channel: RIAs and multifamily offices (Top 300).
   - Secondary Channels: Bank/broker dealer platforms (seventy accounts), wirehouses (Morgan Stanley, UBS, Merrill Lynch), and institutional consulting groups like Graystone.

3. **Plan of Attack:** The sales team will reach out to each account within the TAM to profile their interest in large-cap growth strategies. This will involve:
   - Daily Outreach: Calls, emails, and meetings scheduled for target accounts
   - Profiling: Capturing feedback and gauging interest in the strategy
   - Pipeline Management: Tracking each account in Salesforce, ensuring progress is captured at every stage
   The team will aim to enter a sales cycle with the RIA channel within two years and the platform distributors (banks, broker dealers, wirehouses) within one year.

4. **Tracking and Reporting:** Progress will be tracked through regular reporting, including:
   - Activity Reports: Tracking calls, meetings, and follow-ups
   - Penetration Reports: Showing market coverage across the RIAs, broker-dealers, and wirehouses
   - Pipeline Reports: Organized by the sales cycle, showing where prospects are in the process
   - Scorecards: Monitoring the current status and next steps for each key account
   The account manager will oversee this process, ensuring consistency and accountability.

5. **Optional: Asset Class Study:** To add further context to the sales plan, an asset class study will be conducted. This will analyze how long it has historically taken for similar funds to raise capital, providing a realistic timeline for success. For example, previous studies might

show that large-cap growth strategies typically take twelve to eighteen months to gain initial traction with RIAs, while institutional buyers may take longer.

6. **Reporting Schedule:** The team will report progress every Monday morning during weekly check-ins. These meetings will focus on:

   ○ Performance against the plan.
   ○ What was achieved last week.
   ○ Plans for the current week.

   This level of transparency ensures that everyone stays aligned on the sales plan, progress is continuously monitored, and there are no surprises.

A sales plan like this creates a roadmap that outlines the steps you'll take to achieve success. It answers critical questions, like "Which channels will you focus on? How many accounts will you target? What actions will you take daily to move those prospects down the funnel? And most importantly, how will you measure and report progress?"

The sales plan is not just a tool for organization; it's a protection. It keeps you from being caught off guard when leadership asks for updates. Instead of scrambling for answers, you'll have data-backed reports and a clear record of what's been accomplished and what's next in the pipeline. It keeps you honest, keeps your boss in the loop, and ensures there are no surprises.

Ultimately, a solid sales plan ensures alignment between you and your leadership, providing a shared definition of What Success Looks Like. It turns vague expectations into concrete actions and measurable results, giving you the structure needed to stay on track and manage expectations effectively.

BE THE DOG, NOT THE TAIL

At Dakota, we have weekly check-ins with our fundraising partners. Because our salespeople all create detailed sales plans and report on them daily, our partners have little room to critique us because we can consistently show progress against the plan. As a result, we have enjoyed career longevity as a business, and so have our individual salespeople. Everyone is aligned. Everyone agrees on What Success Looks Like. And everyone can see that progress is being made.

The primary reason I see salespeople struggle is because everything is too loose or completely opportunistic. There are no clear processes and procedures to follow, allowing them the opportunity to become the tail instead of the dog. By putting the first piece in place, Setting Expectations, everything else naturally follows.

Next we will discuss Principle 2: Know Who to Call On.

LEADERSHIP NOTE ON SETTING EXPECTATIONS

From a sales leadership perspective, forcing each individual to write a sales plan and present it in front of the team creates an agreement on What Success Looks Like. This is critical because it transfers the responsibility from the boss to the salesperson and in a natural way makes the salesperson 100 percent accountable for the actions.

3

PRINCIPLE 2—KNOW WHO TO CALL ON

About fifteen years ago, my colleague Joe and I did a sales call with a professional investor. We started off by explaining what we do: we're an active, concentrated large-cap growth manager.

"Well, I only invest in passive large-cap growth," the man said.

"Have you considered active?" Joe asked.

"Yes, but I have chosen to only do passive."

"Well, can I try and convince you of the merits of being active in large-cap growth?"

"No, I'm not interested in active. I only do passive."

Joe went back and forth like this for a few minutes, trying to convince the guy to do something he didn't want to do. It was very unproductive, as you might imagine. In the midst of that conversation it struck me: taking no for an answer was a better route in this case.

After the meeting, I told Joe, "We shouldn't spend our time convincing people to buy something they really don't want to buy. Instead, we should zero in on buyers who already buy what we sell."

This idea has become an essential part of The Dakota Way. While conventional sales wisdom says, "Don't take no for an answer," The Dakota Way recommends the opposite strategy: take no for an answer and move on. Don't be in the convincing business. Instead, find people who want to buy what you sell.

Another core principle at Dakota is we sell apples to apple buyers. Our "apple" is active equity strategies. We shouldn't waste our time trying to convince orange buyers—those interested in passive strategies—to buy apples. We should find more apple buyers and add these people to our prospect bucket. After all, we aren't in the convincing business.

That's really the goal of any investment sales professional: create a bucket and fill it with as many qualified buyers as you can—firms you know invest in your type of investment strategy. Add to that bucket every day. It's that simple.

In the intricate dance of investment sales, knowing your prospect is as crucial as knowing the steps. Knowing Who to Call On is not just about making sales calls; it's about making the *right* sales calls. It's about understanding the nuances of product structure and channel focus to ensure that your sales efforts are not just diligent but also directed.

Knowing Who to Call On ultimately begins with the identification of your TAM, a critical exercise in understanding who the real buyers are. Clarity on your TAM will enable you to tailor your sales efforts effectively, ensuring that you're not simply casting a wide net but fishing in the right waters.

In this chapter we'll define TAM and discuss how to properly reach out.

PRODUCT STRUCTURE DRIVES CHANNEL FOCUS

Your product structure drives your channel focus. In other words, what you sell determines who you call on.

For instance, mutual funds are widely used by RIAs, as well as banks and broker dealers, to create portfolios for their clients. Thus, any fundraiser raising capital for a mutual fund should make sure they get meetings with as many RIAs as possible to explain their investment strategy. At the same time, they should make sure every bank and broker dealer analyst who covers their asset class is familiar with their strategy and is monitoring it. The RIAs have discretion and can make faster decisions, whereas a bank or broker dealer will require a longer due diligence process, but both sales cycles need to move on parallel tracks. The mutual fund product structure drives this multifaceted channel focus on RIAs, banks, and broker dealers.

The mistake many salespeople make is that they call on organizations that do not invest in their particular product structure, as Joe and I did many years ago in that meeting. Someone might really want to call on the endowment at Harvard University, but if their product structure is a mutual fund and that endowment doesn't invest in mutual funds, calling on Harvard would be a waste of time. Instead, find the best-fit channel that uses your product structure.

To Focus on What Matters Most is to find the organizations that consume your type of product structure and investment strategy. Every day, fill your bucket with qualified buyers—and no one else. Don't pursue big brands like Harvard and Yale just because they're big brands. Let your product structure drive your channel focus, and don't waste time filling your bucket with channels that don't want your "apples." Focus your efforts solely on those who want what you sell.

So how do you define the right channel for you? Let's get into it.

DEFINING YOUR TOTAL ADDRESSABLE MARKET

You can think of your TAM as the apple buyers in your bucket who are interested in buying your apples. Keep it simple: identify your best-fit channels and focus on getting meetings with those investors.

It's helpful to get very specific here and identify the number of qualifying accounts in your TAM. For example, if there are three thousand RIAs, you need to know how many of those will actually be interested in your strategy. To help you arrive at this number, you can look at historical allocations and see where each RIA has invested prior and narrow down your TAM to people who buy *exactly* what you sell.

Understanding your product structure and its fit within the market allows you to define your TAM with precision.

This clarity is not just for your benefit but also enables portfolio managers to understand the strategic focus of sales efforts. For example, when questions arise about why funds are not being raised with certain investor segments like endowments, foundations, or public pension funds, a well-defined TAM provides a clear rationale. It highlights the alignment, or lack thereof, between product offerings and potential investors' preferences.

This specificity becomes even more critical when discussing different types of investment strategies. The conversation shifts dramatically when moving from mutual funds to private equity funds, underscoring the importance of targeting the right investors for your product.

Once you've identified your TAM, you know exactly who you're going to be reaching out to. So how do you execute to make progress against your TAM? City Scheduling.

CITY SCHEDULING: A TACTICAL APPROACH

One of the most practical applications of Knowing Who to Call On is City Scheduling. This method is about efficiency and focus, reducing an overwhelming list of accounts into manageable segments. Organizing accounts into metro areas takes an insurmountable task and makes it achievable.

For example, let's say you have determined that the TAM for your product includes RIAs, banks, and broker dealers. Nationwide, that channel totals approximately 2,700 accounts—an overwhelming number at first glance. Break down that total by city, however, and you have something much more manageable. Chicago, for example, might have eighty-five RIA accounts, a number that can realistically be covered in a day or two via individual email outreach.

The City Scheduling approach involves planning meetings in a city three to four weeks in advance, with a structured agenda for each day. Not only does this ensure coverage of key accounts, but it also imposes a discipline that keeps your sales focus on track.

To get started, put a city on your calendar, your notepad, your spreadsheet, or whatever you use to write out your plan. To make the most of the time and get a full day of meetings in, add time slots of 9:00 a.m., 11:00 a.m., 1:00 p.m., 3:00 p.m., and 4:30 p.m. Because you've identified your TAM, you can easily segregate the firms to reach out to in Chicago who fit the channel and strategy that you're selling.

In order to fill those five time slots with meetings, start sending around thirty emails a day three to four weeks in advance. While all of these people won't answer you, they're still seeing your email, seeing your name, and seeing your brand—your outreach is still making an impact. Ideally, the meetings you do schedule will take place in person, but if you are only able to get one meeting in a city, you can always convert to Zoom.

The key to success with this approach is to be scheduling five to ten cities at any given time to keep yourself structured and focused. The goal is to maintain a consistent "asking" process to meet with potential clients across your best-fit channels who are targets for what you're selling.

Now, how do you properly ask for a meeting with your TAM? We've found one surefire way to structure your emails.

CRAFTING THE PERFECT EMAIL

The art of the email is in its clarity. When reaching out to schedule meetings, the subject line should be direct and compelling. For example, "Meeting Request 1/27, 3:00 p.m." leaves no room for ambiguity.

The body of the email should be equally succinct, ideally two to three sentences introducing yourself and your firm strategy, with a definitive call to action. This conciseness respects the recipient's time, and making a specific request increases the likelihood of a positive response.

Here's an example:

Subject Line: Meeting Request January 4th at 3:00 p.m.

Body:

I will be traveling to Chicago with Susan Wilson, President of Sterling Management, on 1/4 and would like to meet and introduce ourselves.

Sterling manages approximately $30 billion in a 22-stock, high-quality, large-cap growth portfolio with weightings between 2% and 8%, where the highest weighting represents the high discount to present value. The strategy has performed in the top decile of its peer group since 2006 with a team that has been together since that time.

Can you meet at 3:00 p.m. on 1/4?

This email packs a punch while being short and concise. By ending your email with a clear call to action, you give the recipient specificity, and if they cannot meet at 3:00, they may say, "No, but I can meet at 2:00."

By sending this email to around thirty people a day, you're likely to book a few meetings. Even if you don't receive a definitive yes, those people still know who you are and what you do.

Your key to City Scheduling and email sending is consistency. The more people hear your name and your brand, the more likely they will remember you down the line, so your next outreach won't feel like a cold call.

DRIVE PURPOSE DAILY

The second core principle of The Dakota Way, Know Who to Call On, sets the stage for a targeted, efficient, and effective sales strategy. It gives you purpose every single day.

Start by understanding your product structure and the channels who are interested in what you sell, and define your TAM as precisely as possible so you know exactly who to call on. Then use City Scheduling and your mastered email to position yourself not just as a salesperson but as a strategic partner to your boss and investment firm.

This chapter lays the groundwork for a sales approach that is focused on the process of identifying and engaging with the right prospects in the right way. Next we will discuss Principle 3, Become a Master Messenger in your meetings with qualified buyers.

LEADERSHIP NOTE ON KNOW
WHO TO CALL ON

In Principle 2, establishing the TAM and creating the email are relatively easy. What is hard for leaders is holding salespeople accountable for City Scheduling. They feel like they are micromanaging.

Newsflash: this is not the case.

If you care about your salespeople, you need to hold them accountable for always scheduling five cities on the calendar at any given time. This simple act will help them consistently make progress against their sales plan and grow their pipelines. You set them up for success and ensure they don't get stuck.

Having this expectation is not micromanaging.

4

PRINCIPLE 3—BECOME A MASTER MESSENGER

Early in my investment sales career I did a great job with City Scheduling in Cincinnati, so I flew in to pitch our partner's strategy at the five meetings. I spent two grand on flights, hotels, and a rental car to get me to those meetings— but I didn't spend enough time preparing for the meetings themselves. Because I had not put in the hard work to take a complicated story (an investment strategy) and make it easy to understand, I did a poor job articulating the strategy. At the end of each meaning, I could tell the person sitting across from me was still confused about what we did, even though I had just spent an hour talking to them about it.

That experience completely changed my relationship with storytelling. It taught me that I needed to master the art.

Investment sales involves long sales cycles, which means you're never calling on the end buyer. That person will have to pitch the product to a colleague, who will have to pitch it to an investment committee, who will have to pitch it to another decision-maker, and so on. You have to make sure the story is easy to understand and easily repeatable.

After those meetings in Cincinnati, I started distilling the core principles of our investment strategy so I could articulate them quickly and clearly, that way my first contact could repeat the same story just as quickly and clearly, and so could every person down the line.

Then I came up with a visual way of explaining the importance of storytelling to my team so they could do the same. This is what I came up with: Imagine that when you sit down with an initial contact, you have a ball of clay sitting on the table between you. You are a professional sculptor of clay, and the person across from you is a professional buyer of clay sculptures.

Who do you want to do the sculpting? The professional sculptor, of course.

The problem is that most salespeople let the buyer do the sculpting, and when they're finished, the ball looks like it was hacked up by a five-year-old kid.

If you have practiced your pitch and have complete control over your storytelling, you can carve that clay into the exact sculpture you're trying to sell, which should be the exact sculpture that person is looking to buy. However, if your message isn't clear and the potential investor is confused to the point of asking basic questions that should have been answered already, the ball of clay gets hacked up into something that isn't what you intended or what the buyer wants. The result is frustration for everyone.

You may have narrowed your target market and filled your bucket with buyers who want your product, but if you can't carve the sculpture so the person sees what you're selling and how they can benefit from it, your pitch will fail.

This chapter delves into the art of messaging, from the opening minutes to the closing questions. It offers strategies to ensure that your message not only resonates but also makes it easy for your prospect to repeat to their decision-making colleagues.

MASTER THE FIRST TWO MINUTES

Now that you've successfully filled time slots in your chosen city, how do you go about your presentation pitch in each meeting?

The opening moments are critical—they set the tone and direction of the conversation. As a fundraiser, your goal is to center the conversation on the key points of your firm and strategy so the prospect knows what they should be listening for.

This isn't just an introduction; it's a strategic overview designed to preempt fundamental questions and establish a solid foundation for the discussion. Key points to cover include:

- The firm's founding
- The firm's location
- Assets under management
- Number of investment professionals
- Strategies managed

- Length of track record
- A unique value proposition
- Client base

Here's an example of a two-minute opening that covers these points:

> Sterling Management was founded in 1998 and today manages approximately $15 billion in one 25-stock large cap growth strategy on behalf of numerous foundations, endowments, corporate and public pension funds, RIAs, banks, broker-dealers, and family offices. Based in New York City, the investment team consists of four portfolio managers and six analysts. The portfolio managers have all worked together at Sterling for twenty-five-plus years. They only manage one strategy, launched in 2010, that can be accessed via a mutual fund and separately managed accounts.

The importance of practicing your opening remarks cannot be overstated. A well-rehearsed introduction ensures that you convey all necessary information quickly and efficiently, allowing more time for in-depth discussion via Q&A. This preparation prevents the meeting from being bogged down by basic inquiries that could have been addressed at the outset.

I vividly remember the hotel in Milwaukee where I stayed during my first fundraising trip after my not-so-successful trip to Cincinnati. This time, I typed out my pitch and practiced it in the mirror, what felt like fifty times, until I had it down. When I was in those meetings, my opening comments flowed. I answered all of the allocators' questions before they even had a chance to ask.

Mastering the first two minutes requires practice. That's one of the activities that matters most in investment sales because it enables you to succinctly address these points and transition smoothly into the core of your presentation, focusing on the specific strategy you're there to discuss.

THE MIDDLE PART: A Q&A CONVERSATION

After your opening remarks, you need to get into a conversation. If you feel nervous, it's easy to launch into a long monologue. Avoid that temptation and instead have a dialogue.

Let the prospect guide you.

I don't mean let them hack up the ball of clay. I mean let them ask questions and then control the conversation—sculpt the clay into the answer they want to hear. If you haven't practiced your message and aren't able to provide that clear, sculpted answer, the prospect will come up with their own interpretations. That's when you end up with a messy lump.

Remember, every prospect has a method to their madness of investing. Likewise, every investment strategy has a story. Your job as the salesperson is to understand the prospect's method and explain the investment strategy's story in a way that the prospect wants to hear it. To aid your understanding, ask questions, and then give short answers to the prospect's questions. This will promote more questions and keep the conversations going.

In preparation for your meeting with RIAs, or any investor for that matter, research their website for their most recent quarterly newsletter. This will show you their current thinking on investing so you can tailor your questions and comments accordingly. Before going into any meeting, you should know exactly what a professional investor wants to know about your investment strategy.

So tell them what they want to hear!

While this may sound a little brown-nosy, I'm here to tell you it's not. The job of a professional fundraiser is to (1) very specifically know the most important information a professional buyer wants to hear about their investment strategy and (2) be able to articulate those exact nuggets of information in an easy-to-understand way.

One question you should ask earlier in the conversation is "Could you please walk me through your investment decision-making process?" The answer will give you a good understanding of how both the due diligence analyst and the firm think about making investment decisions.

This is the art of being a Master Messenger. Set up all the meetings you want to, but if you cannot connect with the buyer and tell them what they want to hear in an easily repeatable way, you are dead in the water.

THE ART OF THE FOLLOW-UP

Once the meeting has come to a close, traditional wisdom suggests that follow-up occurs after the meeting via a series of long emails with PDF attachments. However, nothing could be more wrong. The Dakota Way advocates for a more proactive approach.

If you have been in the investment sales business for a while, then you will be all too familiar with following scenario:

The boss asks, "How was the meeting?"

"Great meeting," the salesperson says.

"Why?" asks the boss.

"Um, um, well, you know, we had a great conversation, they were really into the strategy, and they had some really good buying signals." (At this point I generally want to puke.)

In order for me to not embarrass my team daily with this gibberish, around 2012, I announced, "As of today, we are banning the phrase 'great meeting' at Dakota. If they wired $10 million in the meeting into the mutual fund, then you can say it was a 'great meeting.' Otherwise, tell us the current status and next steps."

At the same time, we implemented a mandatory follow-up technique that does not happen after the meeting but *in* the meeting.

As any meeting draws to a close, we ask the **two toughest questions**. The conversation goes like this:

"Susan, I really enjoyed our meeting today. Do you mind if I ask you a few quick questions? We have spent an hour together, and I think you have a good understanding of our strategy.

"Do you see our strategy fitting into your asset allocation model for your clients?" (Question 1)

If the answer is No, then you know what the follow-up is: mailing list.

If the answer is Yes, then you ask Question 2: "**If that is the case, do you anticipate conducting a search in our asset class within the next twelve months?**"

If the answer is No, you know what the follow-up is: mailing list.

If the answer is Yes, then you ask, "What would be the next steps we could take to begin to better familiarize you and your team with our strategy?"

If you are marketing a private fund that has closing dates, then you would replace Question 2 with "**If that is the case, do you think you would be able to make the March 31, 2030, final close?**" Your follow-up based on their yes or no answer would be the same as before.

These questions are not mere formalities; they are strategic probes designed to gauge genuine interest and potential next steps and avoid the trap most salespeople find themselves in post-meeting: The Unknown.

As a professional fundraiser, asking these two core questions allows you to level set, saving yourself time and allowing you to focus your efforts on prospects who are genuinely interested in their strategy.

By focusing on clarity, preparation, engagement, and strategic follow-up, you can transform your communication from a mere exchange of information into a powerful tool for building relationships and driving success.

This chapter has laid out the strategies and techniques to help you achieve that transformation. In our fourth and final principle, we will review the need for a Killer

Follow-Up System to capture the results of masterfully delivering your message.

LEADERSHIP NOTE ON BECOMING
A MASTER MESSENGER

As a sales leader, it is critically important that you hold each salesperson accountable for asking the two toughest questions to close the meeting. You're actually doing your team a disservice if you don't do this. You're also cheating yourself out of the single greatest time-saving process.

If your salespeople ask these two questions, you know exactly where the company stands after each meeting—whether they'll be moving an opportunity forward or moving on to the next prospect.

5

PRINCIPLE 4—HAVE A KILLER FOLLOW-UP SYSTEM

For many salespeople, follow-up involves keeping track of meeting notes jotted down on miscellaneous sticky notes, in Excel spreadsheets, and on yellow pads. If you've ever tried this "system," you probably know how well it works: not well at all.

To achieve explosive success in the high-stakes world of investment sales, or any sales job for that matter, you need a Killer Follow-Up System in the form of a CRM software.

This chapter explores how leveraging a CRM can 10X your productivity, because you will have rapid, one-click access to the information that matters most to you.

THE POWER OF A CRM

At its core, a CRM is more than just a digital Rolodex; it's a comprehensive tool that enables sales professionals to track meetings they have completed, view call notes, and streamline the sales process.

The transition from 1X to 10X isn't just about working harder; it's about working smarter. A CRM is pivotal in achieving this efficiency, providing a structured and accessible platform for managing sales activities.

Using your CRM properly to track your meetings will create sales triggers, allowing you to quickly act on past meetings. Let's look at four key features of your CRM.

1. TRACK MEETINGS SCHEDULED TO CREATE SALES TRIGGERS

One of the fundamental uses of a CRM is to track your activities—meetings scheduled, calls made, emails sent, and meeting notes taken—over a long period of time, whether it's sixty days, ninety days, or more. This historical data becomes invaluable over time, allowing you to review past interactions and identify opportunities for follow-up or further engagement. It can also automate those sales triggers and set up reminders, ensuring no opportunity falls through the cracks.

Being able to see, with one click, who you have met with and what action is next is indispensable. As I said before, time flies, and if you do a lot of meetings, the downside is that you have a lot of meeting notes. Having a technology to help manage all that data is what makes someone a 10X versus a 1X to 2X salesperson (1X being average).

2. UTILIZE PAST ACTIVITY REPORTS

Once you've tracked your meetings in the CRM, you can run Activity Reports. In case you missed it: these Past Activity Reports are a goldmine of information. They provide a snapshot of your meetings scheduled over a given period of time. By regularly reviewing thirty-day, sixty-day, and ninety-day reports, you can easily identify which prospects need to be followed-up with.

This approach not only ensures that you're consistently engaging with your prospects, but also helps create sales triggers so you can take action. This makes follow-up a natural and systematic part of your routine, and because you can accomplish it within one-click, you are not wasting time looking for information.

3. CREATE AND MANAGE PIPELINE REPORTS

Pipeline Reports, commonly called Opportunity Reports, are another very useful tool for tracking your sales progress. As it sounds, Pipeline Reports are reports of opportunities you have created against an account. Generally the report will include columns such as Firm Name, Opportunity Name, AUM (assets under management), Product, Stage, Account Type, Contact Name, Email, and Phone, with custom text boxes Current Status and Next Steps.

The opportunities should be sorted by Stage with the highest in the pipeline at the top—in other words, the one that is closest to being closed should appear first. By reviewing consistently, you'll be able to move through the list, taking action on those with the most work to be done so the opportunities at the bottom eventually go to the top. Being able to see your opportunities with one click gives you a quick view of the next action steps you need to take without having to think very hard.

If we go back to Setting Expectations, these Pipeline Reports are what you use in your weekly update meetings with your boss. With little effort and not a lot of extra work, you can keep them in the loop.

4. REDUCING TIME SPENT SEARCHING

A significant advantage of a CRM is its ability to save time, a resource as valuable as any in the sales profession as stated in the first chapter. Salespeople often find themselves sifting through notes, emails, and documents, trying to recall details of past interactions or locate contact information. This search is not just frustrating; it's time-consuming and thus counterproductive.

By centralizing all of your sales information in a CRM, you eliminate the need to search through disparate sources. This efficiency means more time spent engaging with prospects and less time trying to remember who they are or what was discussed last. The Dakota Way advocates for this streamlined approach, emphasizing the importance of accessibility and organization in maximizing sales effectiveness.

MAXIMIZE YOUR PRODUCTIVITY

Because of the one-click recall of past meetings with the call notes attached, a CRM is the number one leverage point a salesperson can use to 10X their productivity. This technology should be the backbone of your sales process. We use Salesforce, but there are many other good CRMs for investment salespeople to use, such as Hubspot, Satuit, DealCloud, Backstop, Altvia, and Affinity.

Having a Killer Follow-Up System is not just about persistence; it's about precision. By harnessing the capabilities of CRM, sales professionals can transform their follow-up process from a scattered effort into a targeted strategy that maximizes productivity, from tracking activities and creating sales triggers to managing Pipeline Reports and reducing time spent searching for information.

Remember that the principles outlined in The Dakota Way are not just theoretical concepts but practical tools designed to elevate your sales process.

LEADERSHIP NOTE ON HAVING A KILLER FOLLOW-UP SYSTEM

Many leaders struggle with one vexing question related to follow-up: how tough should you be on your salespeople about entering meetings scheduled and meeting notes into a CRM?

The answer: **very tough**.

Meeting notes are gold bars. The information provides each salesperson with one-click access to their past activities, which triggers sales actions, which is the most important factor in 10X-ing their productivity.

CONCLUSION

One of my most favorite and spontaneous coaching moments happened during my third to last year of coaching, and during my son's sophomore year. Our team stood near the scoreboard waiting to see who would win the league championship. When the scores came out, we saw that we lost by one shot—an entire season came down to one shot. To make matters worse, we lost to our archrivals.

In hockey and lacrosse, the custom is to form a handshake line after each game. In golf, the custom is one handshake after a round, but no line. Seeing a coaching moment, however, I called the team over and said, "Line up, boys. We're forming a line to shake the champions' hands."

"No way," said our captain.

"Please get in line," I repeated.

I then asked the opposing coach to line up his team, and we walked the line shaking the champions' hands.

"Worst thing I have ever done," one player said afterward.

Afterward, I gathered the team by a tree and asked, "Boys, any ideas why I asked you to do that, beyond congratulating them for winning the league title?"

Our captain immediately piped up. "I know why."

"Why?" I asked.

"Because you don't want us to ever feel that feeling ever again."

"Exactly," I said.

Except for our captain, we were a young team that would be together for the next two years. The year after we lost by one shot, we won the league title with a 27–3 record. The year after that, my last year, we won it again, posting a perfect 35–0 record.

Intent is a powerful thing. Those last two years, the boys played with specific intent on what they wanted to accomplish. While the 35–0 record is quite remarkable, the fact that we set that specific goal ten months before the season started makes it even more remarkable.

The team played with clear intent all season to run the table.

Sales is no different, yet it is the one area of business that leaves so many shades of gray regarding potential behaviors to get the job done. There is no Six Sigma of sales like there is in all other areas of business, which makes it difficult to figure out what scalable sales process to use.

This is exactly why I have written this book: to give you one man's approach, with the most clear intent possible, on how to run your sales process and reach your fundraising goals.

The Dakota Way and its four core principles are built with clear intent. When followed, they will, in all likelihood, generate positive results for you and your team.

To cut to the chase, investment sales is hard. Having a proven sales process with only the activities that matter most is critical to success.

This is what I have done with The Dakota Way.

THE DAKOTA WAY

Umbrella Concept: Focus on What Matters Most. For whatever you are trying to accomplish as a salesperson, there are always one or two actions that will have maximum impact. The following principles outline these priority actions.

Principle 1: Set Expectations. Create a sales plan, get agreement on what good looks like, and regularly schedule time to report progress against the plan.

Principle 2: Know Who to Call On. Identify your TAM, create the right email with a clear call to action, and implement City Scheduling.

Principle 3: Become a Master Messenger. Open the meeting with a two-minute overview hitting the key points, move into Q&A on your investment philosophy and process, and end by asking the two tough questions.

Principle 4: Create a Killer Follow-Up System. Pick a CRM, enter all scheduled meetings and call notes, create Activity Reports to create sales triggers, and create Opportunity Pipeline Reports to create additional sales triggers and report progress against your plan.

At the heart of The Dakota Way is the concept of Focus on What Matters Most. This foundational pillar is your guiding light, leading you to prioritize and achieve the most impactful results daily.

Setting expectations is one of things that matters most. When you come to an agreement with your boss about What Success Looks Like, you act like the dog, not the tail. Create the sales plan and set the weekly or biweekly meeting cadence to report progress against your plan.

Identifying your TAM and engaging with your best-fit channels forms the next step in the process, which demands persistence, creativity, and an unwavering commitment to send email meeting requests daily, regardless of what is going on in the markets.

Becoming a master messenger is not an innate talent but a skill honed through practice, practice, and more practice. It's about refining your pitch, connecting with your due diligence analysts, and conveying the key elements of your strategy with clarity. Don't forget to follow up in the meeting. Don't leave the conference room or the Zoom room without the answers to those two tough questions.

The final piece to the puzzle is your Killer Follow-Up System, your CRM, the key leverage point for a salesperson. Getting the meetings scheduled into the CRM for rapid recall to trigger sales actions allows you to 10X your productivity. A CRM is not just about organization; it's about freeing you to be able to quickly focus on the actions that matter most.

TAKE ACTION

Wherever you are in your sales career, embracing principles of The Dakota Way provides a clear path to achieve outsized sales results.

Let's get practical. Go open your laptop, pull up Microsoft Word, and get The Dakota Way started.

1. Write up your sales plan based on the example in Chapter 2.
2. Present your sales plan to your boss and get buy-in.
3. Establish the cadence at which you'll report progress against the plan.
4. Establish your TAM and all the accounts you think you should be calling on—people who buy what you sell.
5. Know and practice delivering your story. Know how to carve the sculpture so people see what you're selling and want to buy it.
6. Utilize the CRM to
   A. Track meetings and notes
   B. Run Past Activity Reports
   C. Run pipeline and opportunity reports

Remember that in taking these steps now, you are not only setting yourself up for explosive success as a sales professional; you are also learning the process that will form the bedrock of your team when you become a leader. As a result, you and your future teams will enjoy lower turnover, less stress, and longer, more stable and fulfilling careers.

PURSUE EXCELLENCE

As we conclude this exploration of The Dakota Way, my hope is that the insights and strategies shared herein extend beyond the pages of this book, inspiring you to pursue excellence in your sales or leadership role. The principles outlined are not merely theoretical concepts but actionable strategies designed to elevate your performance, enhance your dynamics, and achieve your aspirations in any industry.

May this book serve as a compass on your journey, guiding you toward realizing your potential and achieving your dreams through the power of perseverance, focus, and unwavering commitment to excellence.

Good luck as you embark on your pursuit of The Dakota Way, and may your path be marked by success, growth, and fulfillment.

ACKNOWLEDGMENTS

I'd like to thank Gail Fay and Morgan Holycross for their extraordinary effort in bringing The Dakota Way language into this book. Translating someone's voice to written words in an authentic way is no easy task, and our ghostwriter, Gail Fay, did an exceptional job. Morgan Holycross was outstanding in writing, editing, and shepherding the book through the creative process. I cannot thank them enough for their efforts.

I'd like to thank Dan DiDomenico, Tim Dolan, Andrew O'Shea, Ryan Creighton, Tracy Rogers, and the whole investment sales team for their commitment to The Dakota Way and our investment sales process. Their dedication to being exceptional teammates and embracing a defined, consistent approach to sales has the power to be career-changing. Without their incredible support, this book and our business would not be possible.

This book was also made possible through the exceptional, long-term partners who have allowed us to implement this process. I'd like to thank Alan Breed and the entire team at Edgewood for a partnership that has truly been life-changing. I feel like the luckiest person in the world to have crossed paths with Edgewood and to have been part of this partnership since 2006. I'd also like to thank Mark Stitzer and the team at Hamlin who have been partners since 2010. Their trust in us has enabled the growth of their firm and, consequently, Dakota. It has been a remarkable ride, and I hope we all have the opportunity to work together for another twenty years.

ABOUT THE AUTHOR

GUI COSTIN is the Founder and CEO of Dakota. Since its founding in 2006, Dakota has raised over $30 billion for its clients and created a cold outreach database that allows thousands of investment sales professionals to eliminate the administrative work involved in researching who to call on to book meetings.

Gui has one simple mission: to help other people get what they want out of life. Dakota is simply a vehicle to help drive that mission forward.

Prior to starting his entrepreneurial career, Gui earned his Bachelor of Science in Rhetoric and Communications from the University of Virginia. He lives near Philadelphia and is married with three adult children.